secret rooms

poems that challenge domestic violence

TESS BIDDINGTON . JULIE-ANN ROWELL

DANA LITTLEPAGE SMITH . JAMES TURNER

PEBBLE IN A POOL PRESS

First published in 2009 by Pebble In A Pool Press

ISBN:978-0-9561924-0-0

Copyright © Pebble In A Pool Press

Printed by Print Options, Gallows Park, Millbrook, Torpoint, Cornwall PL11 3AX

Typeset in Palatino Linotype

CONTENTS

ACKNOWLEDGEMENTS

Copies of this book are available from 'adva', County Hall, Topsham Road, Exeter, Devon EX2 4QD. Telephone: 01392-382233

Pebble In A Pool Press gratefully acknowledges the support of 'adva' (a collection of agencies working against domestic violence and abuse in Devon) in the production of this book.

Thanks are also due to Maureen Weller for her vital help in the production of this book – layout, cover artwork, and much more.

The poem 'The Door' was first published in the magazine *Fire,* no. 22 2004: 'Dialing Out' in *River King Poetry Supplement* (IIlinois),vol. X,no. 1,2004: and 'Say' in the anthology *Freedom is a Dangerous Word,* ed Brian Edgar, Amnesty International (Exeter Group), 1995.

In violence, we forget who we are.
Mary McCarthy 1912-89

This small volume is the result of a conversation in a café. As we talked, we recognised a theme which resonated with all four of us. The theme found its direction through the work of Tess, who delivers training to raise awareness about domestic violence and its impact.

This impact could be likened to dropping a pebble in a pool. Its effects ripple on through generations, throughout societies, and cause immense suffering. One in three women will experience domestic violence at some point in their lives, which also impacts on their children. Men experience it too, in hetero-sexual and gay relationships, but far less is known about their experiences. What is known, however, is the unacceptable number of women who are murdered by their partners or former partners, who are seriously injured, or whose only escape is through suicide.

However, domestic violence is not inevitable and there are many initiatives that challenge the beliefs that support the use of violence against women. Over-whelmingly, this is something that damages and kills far more women than men.

Tess works for an organisation in Devon called 'adva' – against domestic violence and abuse. Devon has a highly developed response to this issue, ranging from training programmes to pattern-changing courses for women and community programmes for male offenders and much more. A major part of the strategy is ensuring that responses to victims are safe and well-managed. A key agency responsible for this difficult job is Women's Aid, and we would like to donate all profits from the sale of this book to this organisation in recognition of the incredible work that they do.

Tess Biddington ~

Tess Biddington works as a trainer, raising awareness about domestic violence and its consequences. The demands of this work, and caring for a disabled daughter, constitute a large area of her life, but writing is vitally important. She has won a number of prizes for poetry and short stories, including the Bridport Prize, and in 2000, she won the Forward Prize for Best Individual Poem.

PROPHYLACTIC

The treatment can prevent onset of the condition
if taken regularly and before symptoms emerge, reducing
hallucinations, obsessive behaviour and cravings (e.g. for flowers,
white satin, horse-drawn carriages).

Eye tests should be conducted at six-monthly intervals to avoid
the onset of myopia and/or tunnel vision. Distorted perception is common
in the first two years of the illness, but this can be self-correcting
if given enough time.

The manufacturers give no guarantee that the treatment
will be fully effective. Speech/aversion therapy may be necessary
to address the onset of involuntary and repetitious vocalisations, e.g.
'I love you', 'We were meant to be together' and/or 'I want your baby'.

phrases with 'Have you put the bins out?' or 'You never talk to me anymore.'

You should be aware that recurrence can be frequent throughout life.

Store in a cool, dry place

SELF-HELP

I sat up late reading Trauma and Recovery
and the love letters buried, liminal. I saw
I had forgotten the various codes or signs
or at least, they seemed now to have adopted
other, deep-shaft lyrics, wrapped in water.
In pursuit of another dialect, or the old one
refurbished, I turned to the theory of Three Stages.
Number 1: Safety. This I understood, avoiding bare wires,
turning pan handles, testing alarms.
Number 2: Witnessing. More difficult: I stood
kerbside, waiting, hung an invitation around my neck.
People told me my empathy was exceptional: a gift,
they said, as they cried their histories,
their tears smudging the calligraphy on my sign.
I suspected that this was some quirky reversal –
not what was written or intended. Number 3: Reconnection
involved a painful transplant, truly against my wishes.
There are scars which I am assured will fade but
there is no compensation. There is no insurance.
There is no giggle-prevention.

WEIGHT OF WATER

Mother has been drowned.
We saw her face lifting for air
– or so we thought.
Perhaps she was instead

surrendering. Her hair
was beautiful, the way
it took on a slow Eastern grace.
Perhaps it was the hair

that stopped us seeing the desperation

forever and her fingers pressed white
against the glass until it was too late.

Father had her coat ready
pinching the shoulders so the sleeves
hung hopeless and she fell
into its shape. Her shoes are still paired

by the door. I do love you, she said.
We held our forks ready as batons,
glasses of squash quivering in the hope
of Schubert – his fete of fish and streams

returning her to her body
as she laid out plates before us
and we, expectant as a quintet
taking breath before the first chord

drops its pearls into a bow,
waiting for her to say,

      ah listen!

      the piano

      is so much more of a wind instrument.
      Don't you think?

FIRST WOMEN, LASTWOMEN

What is this creature
with insoluble eyes?

That lisps nervously from its
confident length?

We take the fruit, the crisp fracture
of flesh spilling pearls of juice.

See how we dream in sun
our skin alert with breeze.

We cannot know how this dry muscle
can find ease around our throats.

We cannot know how such
tales will throttle us for centuries.

HAIL MARY

My Mother Mary (the Lord is with thee)
at nine years old
drank the holy water for a dare.
What does it taste like? (How the darer coiled his smile
and shuttered his cold eye to a slit as he asked.)

Her finger in her mouth and he explodes:
Mary James, I'll tell on you on you on you!

(How my mother feared the fire.)

Mary Mary (Mary Mother)
how does your garden grow? She pops
the pods; peas into one bowl;
a plague of locusts,
green-winged, light, flightless, in another.

She says, I'll do my penance
at the soil
in the kitchen
beneath my husband
in the purgatory of my unfinished dream
with this row of children
lined up at the altar for the Bishop's thumb.

The silver bells chime sanctus;

incense wheezes from the censer.

Kneel and pray

for your soul Mary Mother, for your bright daring soul

light

bursting out in spears.

Just ordinary, she said. The holy water tasted.

GLOUCESTERSHIRE FLOODS 2007

Marooned a Sunday afternoon
the weather sulking after storms
I listened to the tape.

My father is recording
my younger sister. He wants her to talk about
her visit to the Tower of London. She announces:

The Tower of London has two towers…

He interrupts: No, don't recite it, tell me.

She makes a sound. Not exactly a laugh, more
an uneasy punctuation. And begins again.

He interrupts: Tell me who you sat by on
the coach? She is halted, her concentration washed
away. Just a minute, she says.

I think she is brave to say that to him, but
she was always braver than me. His voice
is smooth like the brown flood.

She begins again. He interrupts: What did
you have for lunch? Her careful navigating

swept away. His voice, softer: Don't lean on the piano.

Julie-ann Rowell~

Julie-ann Rowell's pamphlet collection *Convergence* was selected as a recommended read by the Poetry Book Society. Her first full collection, *Letters North* was published in 2008 by Brodie Press. She has won several prizes and commendations, and teaches creative writing at Bristol University.

NOW YOU HAVE GONE THROUGH THE DOOR

Now you have gone through the door
I've wondered what I should do
where I could take this loss but down to the shore

and its titanic cliffs, the sea's extraordinary blue
so calm, a thousand feet below.
I'd like you to know how these cliffs are hewn –

the zigzag of slate, crystalline granite a flow
of volcanic rock that extends from the Carpathian hills
through Germany, Belgium to the bow

and tilt of Cornwall's fringe, the falls and rills
that carve out its hollows and turns
here where a river takes its time to spill,

sable and strong through a parting of ferns,
splattering with such indifference. This is the place.
There is no other to which I'd rather return.

INTERMISSION

She says she can no longer look at flowers,
The world has closed its covers tight.
The lark, the blackbird and the nightingale
Are empty voices, and day is night,
And night is endless, sleepless, fog and freezing air
      and fright.

She says she can no longer look at stars,
The moon is hidden and the sun blown out.
Curtains hiding every window, bolted doors.
The inside's obscure, all flickering doubt … but
I tell her, the stars will wait, and the flowers; the sun and moon
      will hang about.

THIS PLACE

This is the only place she answers to, these bricks and stone
with scrolling fern, and for luck, a bird's nest in the room,
the slant of light through one window that somehow atones
for this dull day, and adds a lutescent bloom

to table, chair, to mantelpiece. She rests her head,
she confides in herself, the usual rising and falling –
the falling dominates. The trickery of the daytime bed,
the comfort of sheets, that mound of pillows calling.

Easy to be inside and watch the dust clouds play,
the parquet floor stippled with water from her fingers.
A single orchid, pink and white, makes her stay,
as much as the locked front door, the curtain where she lingers.

SPRING AFTERNOON

The day clouded in, so I gave up the idea
of walking under a hangover.

My neighbours were in their garden loudly pretending
to enjoy what should be spring.

The dog dug under the rose bush for the life of him,
as if all useful things were underground.

The rain began just when you telephoned, in tears, to say
you couldn't go on without him.

I think I said, look out of the window for a while,
sometimes the best things come in water.

TOMORROW

Let it be tomorrow not today
the sky is too heavy, thick like clay.

Let it be tomorrow not today
when the trees don't tend to bend and fray.

Let it be tomorrow not today
so I can pretend he's here to stay.

Let it be tomorrow not today
that I have to feel this way.

Let it be tomorrow not today
when I have energy enough to pray.

Let it be tomorrow not today
that there's something left to say.

Then I promise to be good, to listen
and obey.

LISTEN

I called again today to hear your voice,
but you were gone. I knew that you were gone
and yet I hoped for change. I hoped that I
was wrong, that you survived to make a joke
of it, to talk me out of this, the grip
of night, the cool of day. No answer came

to guide me through. I had to hold myself
and talk myself asleep and talk myself
awake. The cure I knew has left me dry
without a sign, without the strength to lift
my heart – that part of me is dead. Listen,
the birds have gone. The sky is thin and white.

GREEN CORRIDOR

The corridor was green she remembers,

pale green that she angled down

feeling her way with tentative fingers,

and white appeared like a shock

in her head, glacial, like the colour of her gown

that she had to wear though it

sewed her in, so she couldn't run

like she did once, where?, in that garden,

which was tame and the grass soft as honeydew melon

that he gave her, it melted on her lips,

the lightest green, but this softness hardened

her. When he talked she could see right inside his mouth.

He was supposed to be helping her change,

but into what? She'd already closed so many doors

and stayed still when he told her to,

swallowed the tablets, allowed the pinpricks.

If only she understood a little more

though he was always telling her to forget.

He smelt of biscuits and sometimes the outside,

but his hands were disgusting,

like something shrivelled in the sun. It's the green

that comes most clear. The green of the corridor

that led to the woman in white like her, who was trusting,

who did not ask the wrong questions, or smile

like the Mona Lisa.

The spill of the heart of the egg onto the bread
and a knife into it. This is how I remember
our mornings together.

Dana Littlepage Smith ~

Dana Littlepage Smith is an American teacher and writer who has lived in the U.K. for the past decade. She has taught street children in Haiti and prisoners in the U.K. and the U.S. She has published two books: *Women Clothed With The Sun* and *Black Elk Dances With Queen Victoria.* Her poetry has received prizes in the U.S. and the U.K.

CLEARED

Who says this fair world is not fair?

For five rare minutes today it seems it is,

as my friend tells me the 'not guilty

verdict' declared for the battered woman

who scattered her husband's limbs to the four winds

and kept his severed head sealed in her ice box.

She called the police numerous times,

told them exactly how the blade had bit,

how the stubble on his chin blued to mould.

But no one believed her. When the penny dropped,

it wasn't because the neighbours missed him.

Nor was it that they saw how the peacock bruises

that bloomed on her face had disappeared.

Rather, they noticed for the first time the dove

grey of her eyes lightened by the palest rim of blue

like Devon skies after long rain has cleared.

STORIES FROM THE NURSERY OF FEAR

This is the man whose fist finds flesh.

And this is his wife whose face turns blue.

Here is the child who watches his father's fist fly

before he runs outside to find a snail

which he will fry with lard – but not to eat.

The boy wants to feel its silent scream.

It's how he makes himself come alive,

he hears flesh curl and spit, razored by flame.

Who will pity the man whose fist finds flesh?

Whose wife weeps, whose child grinds his teeth

in bruised sleep even as he dreams a velvet garden

where snails feast, where bodies unfurl

in dew wet ease knowing it is safe to drink

the sweetness that this world can be.

PERHAPS AT ITS HEART ALL VIOLENCE IS DOMESTIC

Today when I found a girl in the cemetery

hitting her head against the ground,

I touched her ever so lightly and saw

she wasn't crazy. She was simply in desperate need:

homeless, abused and self-abusing.

When we took her in to talk, her face

though smeared with dirt and bruised,

was lit with an intelligence darting and quick

as a kingfisher skimming a river.

And the next morning, when I watched a father

laughing with his gaggle of children, waiting

at the bus stop with them on their first day of school,

I knew the words he used made them feel heart-sure

and happy. Though I didn't speak his language,

I let his words hover round me like a misted

rainbow, endless, yet as basic as a benediction.

Logic is a small fruit and there is much it cannot fathom.

The ways in which each moment is stitched

to the next cannot prove how we may be implicated

in the lives of each other. Yet, if in its conception

all violence is in some way personal and domestic:

each cluster bomb, each rocket, each word

each moment in each day must matter.

For it will be in this world and no other

where I recognise each stranger as the beloved.

SLEEP, EAT, SLEEP

With the small stones it takes three…

she pauses and I ask,

'Hours, days?' Her husband

shakes his head to disagree.

He has more words than his wife.

Although she has seen what the world

can do, she has more faith.

He continues, 'Our law states

a woman must be caught in adultery

by her husband, father, uncle, cousin,

son, so…' He shrugs and smiles,

'You can see, it never happens.'

Except it does, every day, his wife,

my friend does not need to say.

When he leaves she leans into me,

My blood – she drags her fingers

over her veins – *it feels so spicy!*

He says to me: sleep, eat, sleep.

I tell him I am not a cow.

What I want to eat is kindness.

Yesterday, I went to my closet

with all the clothes he buys,

I throw them in the street.

What is happening to me?

Write this please -

with no names in

and slip it under my door.

Maybe then I can know

what something in this life means.

HEALING IS THE SLOWEST ART

This time it isn't the head under the carpet,
or the mouldering torso in the shed, armless
because she never needed arms, we kept her
that passive… Nor is it the dead fish thickening
like a tree stump in my mouth. No, this time it's
the elephant I'm easing off my shoulders.
Its skin is thick and scarred as shame,
like the family heirloom passed down
through generations which we were taught
never to mention. But don't be fooled,
don't think this will be a simple manoeuvre,
the bend at the hips, the knee angled so as not to be
crushed. Getting out from under this much rotting meat
is a subtle art, as difficult, almost, as hoisting the leviathan aloft.

EXPLAINED

The picture is of a naked girl.

Above all, she is perfectly –

the rest is contrivance & shadow.

Note the eyes as she confronts –

as if she is simply having.

The main ingredients are chains

and flesh, the shadow of a shadow.

Power is leashed, but its spiked

collar makes each participant grovel.

Pardon me if this sounds obvious –

but nothing here is play or done for

play. Here, even the brutal cowers.

I JUST WANT TO FEEL SAFE

My friend tells me the blackbird learns a phrase for life

and when it dies that particular glissade, that trill of life

that joy rush of notes that spill through the sky,

disappear. Tonight while I sit in my garden beneath

deep bellied clouds of dove grey with my glass of wine,

I hear a woman cry: *I just want to feel safe,*

you've taken all my medication.

You've taken all my money…

And still the blackbirds sing—

James Turner ~

James Turner, retired library assistant, lives in Exeter. For five years he co-hosted Uncut Poets, Exeter's poetry venue. His poetry collection *Forgeries* is published by Original Plus.

THE DOOR

Somebody sawed part
of his memory off
when he was a kid. Ever since then

he's had to think on crutches.
Who was the carpenter?
One day he'll remember

a hand
on the back of his neck
pressing his face into a pillow.

A taste of terror
speading forward along his tongue
like vomit.

Suddenly being able
to lift his head and
stare into the darkness.

And light, flooding the room
then fading to darkness again
(that must have been the door

letting somebody out).

DIALLING OUT

You dialled my number – nothing. Fear
is a clothes-line slung across your life
from end to end. You walk it as
a tight-rope but every time you fall

it somehow falls with you, always
under your feet so you never hit
the ground. When you're asleep the Devil
hangs his washing on it. The patterns
on his T-shirts are your dreams:
last night you were a girl again,
your father's pet, and felt his hands
stroke your hair, and heard his voice
say how handsome you were, and saw
on his lips that smile that meant so much
to him as it pushed your protest under.
He took a big black bulldog clip,
clipped it on your hair at the back
and let you go. You walked away,
unsteady, sick with unshed tears,
sensing his eyes on you. Then you

couldn't get through to me because
the phone box you were dialling from
was swinging high up from a crane,

and in your hair the bulldog clip

and through the glass his eyes still on you.

BRUSH THE WOUND

with soft insistent questions. Open the door
to the secret room, let in some air and light.
Observe the footprint in the dried mud. Listen
but don't believe it when they say no foot
trod there. Start a new year freed-slave.
Trust your own compass needle. Learn
to steady when the needle settles. Breathe
your biggest fear away. Let the story
of your life unfold. Let the footprint speak. Let
the long-locked room stammer out its secrets.
The music of truth will tell you what to feel
like the soundtrack of a film. Decode the shapes
in the sand. Let genius be your companion. Listen.
Do not believe or merely repeat or follow
Dostoievsky, Shostakovich, Goethe,
Krishnamurti, but read what their mirrors reflect
of what's been too long hidden in your heart.
Or forget the books and the music, forget great art,
and let two people sit down to talk, as friends,
unhurried, without the pressure of persuasion.
Brush the wound with soft insistent questions.

SAY

Say there were no such thing as truth
but only your word versus mine;
say crowing victors were correct
and victims wrong because they whine;
say there were no such thing as truth,
just rebels and the party line:

you'd lick your story into shape
till I believed it with my eyes –
your telling it would make it so –
you'd gag the baby when it cries,
you'd lick your story into shape,
and there'd be no such thing as lies.

DEMOCRACY

When I was a boy
I said to my friend
I hate people who hate.

Not that I thought they should fry for it.
I wanted to be a good man,
not just vote for the right party.

I've never been fanatical
about democracy
but it means more to me
(gives me more, that's why)
than it did to women and slaves
in ancient Greece

or to the Navaho woman
who sold me a bit of patterned cloth
near the rim of the Grand Canyon.

We hold these truths
but what use is democracy
to you as a kid
if you can't vote to stop
what daddy does to you sometimes?

SONG

The meek kid clams, mud-stuck,

the germ of it cooped with ma and pa

in the sob-rife wit's-end grid

of his no-roam mad-bad ashram-home

where simply to be means railed-at, nabbed and tarred

is the spiritual lesson

that will fuel his later woo-loop skids

into second-chance love-shop failure.

No cure, no sop in the waver

of this all-same short-life stutter of a song

where simply to be is a ticked-off sin

is the sad refrain

you retain when its lesson's over.

GEORGE DEFINED

in an equation of darkness, as a chunk
of undifferentiated experience, beyond measure.
He told you his childhood worst didn't he? which he
remembers remembering thirty years later but can't
directly remember. His brain is a quantum jungle:
photons arriving at the retina set
the palm fronds swaying like palm fronds, as if Exeter
possessed its own secret Botanical Gardens
with friendly Rousseau lion to rip you apart
and a great half-moon hanging in the afternoon
like a slice of watermelon. He told you the repeated
rape didn't he? which he was cleverly trained
to submit to in silence as if it were friendly intimacy,
then to keep silent about it after and always.
He told you the giant hand didn't he? that pushed
his face hard down into a softness of pillow,
stopping his breath. That hand spoke absolute power.
From this he concluded that he couldn't be human.
It may be too late now to help him change this belief.
George will have to penetrate deep, deep into
his jungle, to journey far, far back into
his unwriteable biography before he can see
that he's made of the same stuff as everyone else.
It's the sudden darkening of the expression
in a nearby friendly face that terrifies him.